Writing to Reach You

Willow McGlashan

Writing to Reach You © 2022 Willow McGlashan

All rights reserved.

No part of this publication may be reproduced, stored in a retrieval system, or transmitted, in any form or by any means, electronic, mechanical, photocopying, recording or otherwise, without the prior written permission of the presenters.

Willow McGlashan asserts the moral right to be identified as author of this work.

Presentation by *BookLeaf Publishing*

Web: www.bookleafpub.com

E-mail: info@bookleafpub.com

ISBN: 9789357448031

First edition 2022

DEDICATION

To Sissy and Rio, who inspired and encouraged me, and to Caroline, who gave me courage and guidance.

ACKNOWLEDGEMENT

Cover photo credit to Sheng Li on Upsplash

PREFACE

This collection of poems is loosely based off of dreams, with the titles corresponding to when it was written. Most of the poems have very little to do with the author's real life, but are still very closely correlated to her personal experience.

20.18.05

You still think you know why I'm here
Balanced on the spine of the world
Above the ocean
It's sea, salted, baltic, full
Of stories no one has ever told
Many that have been said
Few that have ever been listened to.

I always listen.
Maybe that's why i'm here now
Pockets full of sadness and sand dollars.
There's no way you know why I'm here
I'm not quite sure myself.
Maybe the moon and I are friends
Maybe I come here to listen
To stories no one else hears
Or maybe to tell a few of my own.

I tell you that I am home
Within myself and that the wind
Is also a friend of mine
And has been for a long long time.
It took a long time for me
To find my home. I've already been
sitting on the seafloor for a long time
And I am not about to jump.

20.22.06

We late night rendezvous
Behind a scrap-metal bike shop
in the city centre,
Your teeth in my soul.
The stars look nice tonight
In your eyes and in the slice
Of sky from a gap in the cereal-
Box tenements, in this alleyway
I tell you more about the stars
Our home, and how we never really
Know quite where we're headed.
Listening with a lemon-segment smile
In your mouth, I know
That this helps you more
Than it helps me.
I hear the loneliness behind all the
Tell me more's and
What's that like's and
I watch your broken-glass eyes
Fill up from the inside with light
Instead of just reflecting streetlamps.
It hurts a bit, this vulnerable storytelling
Slicing off bits of my soul to butter for you,
But I know you don't have many stories you can tell

And you're hungry always
So I'm back every week with a grocery list
Of tales to tell, pretending
That I don't worry the next day
That this story finally scared you off;
Oversharing how afraid I am
That you see more every day of who I am
And who I'm trying not to be.
But it's easier to share with a stranger-
To pretend to myself that you're a stranger-
Than to share with anyone I see more
Than once a week.
Sometimes the only reason I'm still around is
Because I can see how my stories
Fill you up and so I meet you
Every Wednesday by the convenience
Store with stories and sandwiches
To digest as we walk to the bike shop.
I tell you about the time I dyed my hair
Strawberry ice cream,
About how the moon came to be,
About what excitement tastes like to me,
And I watch as your voice bleeds
From rust into peach sorbet.
I walk you back one block over
To an empty apartment.
I ask in a shrug
You reply with a shrug
Da's working late. See you next week?

A hug that feels like rice paper and pretzel salt.
Then I dissolve into dusk and solitude
As I head home to sleep and
The city wakes up around me, ravenous,
Prepared to chew me up and
Spit me out again tomorrow.

20.15.08

There is a shipwreck between your ribs
and it took eighteen years
for me to understand
how to understand your kind of drowning.
There are people who cannot be held
quietly. There are screams
that are never externalized. If I looked
at the photo albums of your
past twenty years, all I would find
are decibel meter graphs of
phone calls and the intensity of your silence
as you sat smoking cigarettes in the garage.

There is a shipwreck between your ribs
and glass in your fingerprints. You are
a box with fragile written on it,
and so many people have not handled you
with care.

And for the first time, I understand
that I will never know
how to apologize for being
one of them.

20.30.08

Press your hands into the soft velvet crush of sky above you,
and catch the stars like sequins beneath your fingertips.
When will you realise that this feeling of wonder in your soul when you look at the stars is the same
as the one I get when I think of you?
So rich I feel sometimes I might suffocate from the flowers in my lungs,
or crush my pastry heart, strawberry
and crumbling in your hands. I look at the stars, and see the silver of your eyes, the quiet in your tired smiles.
I look at the stars and see their beauty, yes, but also
everything we could ever be, all that you could become, and
I wonder how there is space for me beside you in this sky.
I feel paper thin and flammable next to your sunlight,
and wonder that you consider me an equal.
Someday- not tonight- I'll tell you that you saved my life,

and my hands won't shake when I say I love
you.
I think it has always been true, but I cannot
admit it just yet. Of course, I will have to leave
then,
for I am no galaxy, and you will never
look at me like you do the night sky, but I will
always
see the stars and know the hidden edges of your
grin,
and the easy slip of your palm in my hand.

20.13.09

An amaranthine sunrise
splits the sky open, juicy and overripe,
and the light catches between your
teeth as you grin at me.
The tops of the mountains are jagged
and toss us up for a gaping maw
of space to swallow whole. The horizon
burns orange, sunny side up
and flecked with pepper birdsong
and I feel my ribs
ache with molten joy.
The sheer querencia sits
heavy in my stomach, stretching
the time around us.
Taffy:
just as sweet,
just as sticky.
You chew back a laugh and remind me
not to choke on my
thoughts. I reply
that there will never be
another sunrise like this one.
A pause.
A slow blink.

You look back out at the puréed sunrise
with new perspective glinting in your
eyes; I watch you
watch the sky and
make a memory.

20.02.10

The night staggers under the
weight of snow and
hungry birds die of frosted bellies. Snow is
beautiful, wonderful, and
on all nights except this one it
feels safe and familiar.
Tonight it
tastes like hypothermia. Tonight, it
is a creature, no longer
a condition but
alive, sentient, eating bird skeletons
and souls indiscriminately. Tonight, you
feel like running through it
barefoot, coatless,
unhindered and frozen and raw. Feel the ice
cut ribbons through your feet and cry
redemption for the blood on
the ground, the blood in
your mouth, blood leaking
from your heart.
Instead you bruise ink
into your notepads— stain
your fingerprints and imagine
candles snuffing out, imagine
burning out until

you can curl up in the icy morning
sunshine and exsanguinate waxy
disappointment into the snow.
Leave an impression to be
cast or cast aside. Nothing
is worth the weight of this world,
and nobody has learned how
to bear it alone. You will
die trying.

20.10.10

I feel like a sometimes-child today,
all lost opportunities and hypotheticals.
I kick pebbles in the back of the playground
and avoid eye contact. Can you still hear me?
Will you listen?

It's been a week and a half since
 I hugged someone and my
bones feel ashy and brittle. I
left my water bottle at home and
now I'm starting to levitate. I want
to exist on stardust and chamomile tea
but I have food in the fridge
on the verge of expiration
so I have to stay at least until
it's all gone. I can hear the fridge
humming. It's an old pop song today.
You have to listen to hear it, right?

At work today I saw myself talk
to someone else and wondered
why I couldn't hear anything.
The world is starting to go fizzy
at the edges and I wish it would
dissolve faster. When the universe

comes calling for me give him my number.
I'm free every Tuesday after four, if he's
listening.

Last week I woke up at seven
and was out of my bed at half past three.
I went for a walk and the clouds
were mash-potato-ed and heavy
with snow. I'm walking past the mountains
and walking further. Would you notice
I'd left you behind? I'm planning to hitchhike
to Venus, and I took your guitar, the one
with the broken string. I hope
you don't want it back, I'll need it
to busk for money I'll spend on coffee I don't
drink.
I wonder if they'd trade me
a sandwich for a song.
Would they listen?

If I told you all
of the heathery thoughts in my brain
would you still be comfortable
spending time with me? I'm not
anything extraordinary, and I look a little
too longingly at the sharper silver in the
kitchen. You might not ever get me to believe
anything good you tell me of myself,
but everyone is allowed their own

opinions and you can think whatever you want.
I only have one number saved to speed dial.
I don't let myself stand alone near edges
anymore.

20.28.10

The rain plummets earthward
and the clouds roil, revolting
against the idea that you
are honest with yourself

Storms make us more honest.
I think it's because in the quiet
of a calm day we can hear
ourselves think and we censor
ourselves from saying anything
vulnerable.

I think it's because in a storm
the world is so
vast around us, and
we are utterly at it's
mercy. If I die,
we think, at least let this
last thing be said.

Never mind that we are inside and dry.
Never mind that the rain is no more
dangerous than the cold we will
catch from it.

Never mind that all our bad decisions
will be here to regret tomorrow.
Right now, we
are alive, and the storm is
raging, and you are afraid.

And still, you lie. I can see it
in the tightness of your mouth
as you sip from the tin of fizzy juice
I passed you. I can taste it
in the way you blink too sharply, and
I want to hold your
hand but
you are lying to me still and so
I am not allowed.

20.17.11

There are some wounds that don't heal
And the rawed edges of them grate
and rasp against each other
Long after the skin has smoothed
and outside eyes can't see
The weeping shards still cut your lungs up
Some things will never return.

Gone. GONE. Hit the ground
and scream murder at the stars.
They cannot hear you. Nothing will return.

The life of this memory is gone forever.
Cry and the salt stings your cheeks.
It will never soothe you, and
the red chafe on your cheeks from
scrubbing them dry sits like an angry blush.
The memories continue to bleach
with every revisit they deteriorate
and cut another slow hurricane bruise
into the spongy parts of you. Things like these
cannot return, and there are no good substitutes.

grief manifests as fatigue

anger weighs like a wooden blanket
sorrow pulls you down to jagged ground
hoping for something to distract you
the way only splinters can
dig nails into your palms cut crescents
suck the blood from your teeth and
bind your knuckles and your heart up
tightly to stop the bleeding, the thoughts
circle won't stop won't still won't cease won't
and it needs to stop and I'm too dizzy for
help and sometimes irreplaceable things don't
return.

Sometimes, peace tastes like pomegranate seeds;
the colour green; wearing new shoes; staying up
thinking till the sky turns grey
Sometimes when the mirror reflects just right
a stranger can look hauntingly familiar
Sometimes, being alone under the stars
looks like salt and blood
Sometimes, a gust of wind seems
to rip through the hollow places that you
thought were healed, and you stop
in the sunshine to breathe and remember.
What you miss will not return, and won't be
replaced.
This doesn't hurt as sharply as it used to.

20.06.12

September has no lungs
I talk to her when the sky is dark
And sometimes she'll meet my eyes
And the warm dirt sighs and
Flowers will relax their rosebud fists
Leaves sink through the moonlight
and stars think, i know what that
Feels like too, syrup and luminance.

You tell me you love them in October and
The breeze chokes and sputters snowflakes
Dead leaves spin at your feet like a ghost town
Where skeletons clutch anything beating
Close to themselves, muttering
Why can't i breathe, why am i never breathing.

This is an in-between-space
A forest of powdered-sugar tree trunks
Animals hide beneath the slow warmth roots
And I wish I had brought a scarf
November seems content in its decay
And shrugs at my complaints
But scrubs my cheeks dry as I trudge home.

December rises and shakes his head

And says it's been a long time coming
When the world stops spinning
Snow settles in blank drifts and decides
That it will be here to stay
And things I wish you had said to me
Look blue and flimsy in the early dusk
And I think less and less of them and you.

20.19.12

I almost miss the sound of your voice
but know that the rain
outside my window will suffice for tonight.
I'm not drunk yet, but we
haven't spoken in months now
and I wanted to tell you that
someone threw a bouquet of
roses
into the bin on the corner of my street
and I wanted to cry
because, because —
well,
you know exactly why.

I guess I'm calling because
I knew you wouldn't answer. I guess I'm calling
because only you would understand
how that would break my heart.

I'm running out of things to say.
My petrol is running on empty.
I've stopped stealing pages out of poetry books
but last week I pocketed a
thesaurus and looked
for synonyms of you

but I could only find
rain and more rain
and a thunderstorm that
sounded like glass
like crystal
like an orchestra.

I wanted to tell you
I'm not afraid of being moved anymore,
of feeling world-vast and
molten in the middle,
of this heart packing up
and flying transcontinental
with only a woolen coat and a pocket
with folded-up addresses inside.

I've saved up enough money to disappear.
I know you never
thought the day would
come.

Do you remember when
we said goodbye and
promised that
it was only for then?
It's been years
since I last saw you, centuries
since we last spoke.

Sometimes, it gets quiet enough
that I can hear the cicadas creaking out
rasped threats against each other
in the balm of a night that tastes
of ice-lolly sticks
and bruised kneecaps

I've forgotten almost everything
about you already, except that
the skin of your hands was soft
like the belly of a peach
and how you would laugh,
making fun of me
for the way I pronounced almonds
like I was falling in love
with the language.

21.05.01

I saw you
in a purple hoodie and blue jeans
that looked like the ones you wore
when we picked rosehips
and I saw you
in the crossed ankles and
the curly hair, sunlit and dark
you are oceans away
too many heartbeats apart
from where I am.
she looked at me with a squint and
I realised I was staring
realised staring would not
make you come home to me
I walked a little faster
apologetic when I went past

grief is a silver pin
and it twists itself deeper into a person
catching on the soft parts and
aching sinews.
A thasgaidh,
you would have scoffed
at the pieces of my heart I chipped off
for you

because the other alternative is tears
and I never want to make you cry
it's better to laugh
over something that weighs like the ocean
than to look at what it is
you're holding in your hands.

21.03.02

I saw the phrase 'lemon lime spine'
on a post about how
things that take us by surprise
are ones that make us laugh.
The author meant it as nonsensical
but I heard that phrase and thought
of the bubbles that trace themselves
across my ribs and down my back
whenever you laugh.

lemon lime, sprite
carbonated laughter and summertime
days with your warm palm laced against mine
a hand against my spine after I stumble
these are things I think of
when I think of you.

If I focus on it
all I see is how perfectly
lemon lime describes you
I think of the tang in your smile after a good
joke
the green tones of chlorine stain
from that time we spent the whole day in the
pool

and our shoulders were strawberry for a week
afterwards
I think of how easy you are with new people
of effortless conversation and easy jokes
how you would elbow me and repeat their
names
into my ear till I could remember them myself.

You took me by surprise in the best way
any time I spent with you
ended dizzy with laughter
and drunk on affection
happiness in bursts like the release
of pressure from a fizzy juice tin.

But pressure can build too much
and carbonation gradually flattens.
Bubbles leach into a sugary stagnation
of feeling I cannot manipulate
knowing that at some point
I became the one who was
shaking you until your bubbles died.
It broke my heart.
You, sprightly laughter and cheer,
someone unhappy because of my handiwork,
letting you go was a small price
to pay for the gift of honest friendship
and keeping you alive.

I still love you sometimes
in the quiet moments of lazy afternoons
but these are fewer and farther away
than they used to be
and I am learning to let go.

21.06.04

i wanted to be a creator
but creativity plays second fiddle
to survival
everything i've ever left behind
has claw marks gouged through it
the same way we leave
handprints of paint on the walls
for millennia to fade and
our children to find
and know: we were here
i was here- i have fought
and carved out spaces
for myself to live
for centuries
my battle is eons old
told and retold
worn thin and brittle
and desperate with
the need to survive
to outlast
to be known
my hands talon
with intent and carve
what i want to be remembered as
into the rock of my skull

i rock back and forth
back
and forth
the ebb of sea tides
erodes stone and
my
fragility, mortality, anxiety
crashes over me
blinding in salt and pressure and froth
shaving away the sharpness of my
desperation
for survival, for legacy
how can anyone create
without having anything to say
who has the courage necessary
to expose the softer parts of themselves
again and again
to the scrutiny of predatory gazes
and recover each time
i would love to be a creator
but all of my willpower is
focused on surviving past tonight.

21.14.04

Home is a pretty colour on you,
it always has been. Look at
the sunshine flush in your cheeks
and the sweet grace in your movements.
I can see the way this land loves you.
I can see the way green steals over
the ashy branches you hang from,
the way parched grass springs a little
livelier after you pass.
This breeze is going out of its way
to kiss your forehead and tug at your sleeves.
It's trying to hold your hands
and beg you to stay.
A million I-love-yous in every motion,
in every wave of greenery an intention-
a coercion and a plead- appealing for
the barest moment of audience with you.
I see you reach easily for a dying
blossom, cinnamic and crisped dry.
You pluck it and twist it into your glossy hair.
I can almost hear the other flowers
sighing something about your courtesy
and kindness. In the puddle of darkness
under this cherry tree, the clouds above us wink
a suggestion of stars

and I listen to the branches creak as they
shift against the wind to keep
the sunlight from hurting your eyes.
Yesterday in the stream
the cold water burbled easily around your ankles
and softened the stones specifically for you,
so that your steps would be easy and carefree.
My point is: this land loves you
loves you in it
needs you here
wants you to stay.
Do not ever feel like an imposition-
an imposter, an outsider- it is an offence
to every soul-ed being in this valley.
I can see too
the way you start to lighten as you
spend more time here in your home.
The drain on your vibrancy is gone
and I can see sunset colours pooling
underneath your skin
and flushing beneath your cheeks.
Let your home
settle back into your bones,
let the dirt bury your grief
and wash the aches from your soul.

21.18.04

look at me, listen to what
I tell you: this is a glass-blown
moment that you're trapped in

watch closely
do you see what I mean
it glows

humming with warmth and dripping
sunshine over everything, and you
think of summertime, of campfires, of sand

now think of a glass blower's kiln
see the heat
see the molten glass being rolled

in a billion memories
see those experiences melt into this
amorphous, fluid emotion

watch the spin as it glows and drips
punch drunk with novelty and
dizzyingly bright and now

watch
see it fill
watch it expand and

look at what it shows you
see the physical world shrink
sunshine blasting everything out

except the one you love
can you see them smile
can you see them molten on the inside

it's what's inside you that's ballooning
watch your soul inflate
with so much emotion that you

can hardly breathe
feel your lungs glow
your hands are holding stars

the sky careens away from you
a giddy mess
lurching haphazardly into nothing

it's wonderful
terrible
soul-shatteringly terrifying

to realise that the person you love

reciprocates with just as much fervour
now you need to do something

it feels a lot like being drunk
like being underwater
like being blown from glass

especially the last one
sugar thin and delicate
fragile and luminous

hearts are flighty things and
it's dangerous to give yours away
unless you trade equally, as an exchange

carry the beating-heart softness
of a fledgling emotion in your hands
and resolve not to let it drop

make a promise and see
the smile glimmer in their eyes
and save this moment.

21.30.04

With a sort of muted terror in my lungs
I watch through the window as
I tear my life apart
feeling set aside and distant
someone else
looking through sugar paste
at a life I don't belong to.

Surely that isn't me
I say
peering through the glaze
surely I would not be enough
of a fool to intentionally sabotage
the things that mean the most to me.

And yet here I stand as a stranger
watching myself self destruct
jade and apathy dripping from my elbows
onto the floor from the chair
in front of my laptop
a little black cursor mark
blinking balefully from an empty page.

Here I sit
watching the blank document tick

closer to an impending deadline
and still I'm unable to write
what I want to say
and I'm hopeless enough
to consider quitting.

Stagnant
sustained in a moment
unable to move
while the world speeds up around me
have I eroded into amber
or dissociated into this reality I'm stuck in.

I do not want to stay here
I have work to do and sleep to wish for
and yet I cannot physically move
to achieve what i need to
i cannot mentally process
what I need to do
and I think I might cry
from the weight of the guilt I feel
over my uselessness
and wasted time.

21.15.05

Sometimes the world
suspends itself for just a moment
cars still pass and the world moves
in colour and sound around us but
right now there is only an existence

there is only you
sat on the sidewalk with our bags
in your lap and a melting ice lolly
lining your wrist with red
there is only me
stepping into the street
with a camera in my hand to catch
the pink wisps of sunset clouds
as they dissolve into the darkness
and stars above the city

I watch the edge of the sun
limning gold stitches into the sky
i'm ignoring the sharp bits
of thought that twist and demand
i stay until a car comes by
too fast and shatters the moment
over the edge of the world

The air glows golden
bell clear and liquid
molasses around us as
this instant hovers in suspense
and for a second everything feels fine

The anticipation is a drug
it's the moment before the
fall on an amusement ride
and i can see the edges of your
smile by the way your eyes crease

I cannot be the reason you fall
so i step back onto the pavement
and wait for you to gather your feet
beneath yourself
limbs akimbo
long unruly angles as
you juggle your treat and our bags
and get ready to go home.

a car passes with headlights
that look like freedom
far enough away that
only my jumper is displaced
by the gust of wind as it goes

i catch myself wishing i had stayed
for another half minute

i just need time
i cannot let go while you
want me around
i cannot let you closer while i
want to disappear
you will tire of waiting before long

when the time comes that you've
replaced me with a photoprint and memories
i will be ready to let
the timelessness of a lost feeling
and moments like these
suspend me for long enough
to step over the edge of the world

21.22.06

It sounds like the end of the world-
all quick wind sharp stones,
fall, gall yourself, gash gold
and wish the world would end.
Ichor is dripping from
the ends of your fingers
where you pulled yourself back up
over the edge of the mountains
where the world bleeds ochroid
rust as the sun dies.
Everything does eventually
and you are no exception.
I am no exception and time is short.
Prepare yourself before all you have is
denial and missed opportunities.

It's the end of the world:
the crash of rotting metal as rust
crawls through the foundations
of what I thought we'd built
to last forever.
The sound rolls over the land around us-
Can you hear it echo
or is it only in my mind?
I am no exception to the end of the world

and neither are you.

It sounds like we're underwater;
like we're breathing with the fish;
like the end of the world.
I thought we'd have more time and
my hubris became denial.
I'm choking on the words I wish I would've said,
the ones I was saving for a better time,
and now it's the end of the world-
the end of us- and
I'm out of time to tell you
how I feel.

21.21.09

Sea salt
squinted eyes in a creased face like cracked leather
lowered brows against the brooding sky
wind lashes the ropes against the deck
my Granddad stood at the prow
of a ship older than he was
and looked into the vast cold of
a wide ocean older than imagination

Over the swells came this swift
gull-canny vessel
fish-full-pelican bobbing through waves the size of the world
flaking grey paint like scales and the flash of yellow-beak bow
when the sea breaks around itself and somehow
in the grey and the gloom and the wet, wet-salt sadness
and anger of ocean fighting itself in an eons-old repetitive argument
This speck-wee ramshackle ship moves like it is made from sea itself
under the skilled, driftwood and riveted hands
of someone land-born but

ocean raised
as much north sea native as any guillemot
as much seaweed-fluid motion as any seal

Granddads eyes are squinted black in his craggy face
dripping with rain and seawater indiscriminately
sopping jacket and wellies that squeal.
Reaching harbour,
there is a practiced leap to the land
and the awkward gait of someone
unused to the jarring steadiness of loam
greets him like an uncomfortable acquaintance
i recognise his goose-stoop knees and
the shift of his weight as though he expects the sea
to reclaim her ground
and shred the tarmac beneath his feet into seafoam

The hearth fire is a crackle of merry driftwood
and to me it means biscuits-and-tea,
thick treacle slathered on a piece,
and stories
A tea towel drops over my head to stop the
dripping from the ends of my hair on the carpet
and Granddad sits down across from me
the firelight catching in his weathered face
a foil to the rain outside

dripping into his eyes and lighting them aglow,
glinting off his teeth and he grinds out
tales in his gravel voice
of sea monsters and myths
he gestures through his tales and flings
more than one biscuit into the flames on
accident
i watch as his energy makes the little discs flame
into carbon.

21.04.10

being stuck in this dream is
making me feel like the world will never end
and like the world is ending too quickly
curtains up, stage set
this reality is not mine and yet
i am here and i want to go home please
stage-lit ambiance paints us
here at the kitchen table with
your homework and a
half eaten apple between us
i have not moved in three hours
i stare into space and memorise
the crook of your elbow
you have not noticed and
it makes me think that this is not real
and that i am not here i am dreaming.
the table bursts into flames and now
i am certain that i am not
actually existing here, this is a dream
and so i let the flames lick up my arms
i pillow my head in my hands
and wait for the quiet dark of early morning to
wake me up
In the darkness there is the soft
breaths of sleep and a warmth in the blankets

that tugs me back down despite the wind
tugging at the windowsill yelling to be heard.

Milton Keynes UK
Ingram Content Group UK Ltd.
UKHW021855230824
447235UK00012B/473

9 789357 448031